# Happenstance Farms
## Catch That Pony

Written by
S. McMichael

**HAPPENSTANCE FARMS BOOKS**

www.happenstancefarmsbooks.com

*Printed in St Louis, MO*

# This book is dedicated to

*All the sassy ponies and determined girls who have learned so much from them.  Also, the Trainers who provide a safe environment for the ponies and riders to learn.*

"Come on, Sophia!" Savanna called. "We're going to miss Ms. Ellen's surprise!"

Sophia picked up speed, easily passing her friend. "Way ahead of you!" she shouted.

The girls slowed their pace when they saw Ms. Ellen up ahead. Beside her was the cutest pony they had ever seen.

"Wow! Just look at her," Sophia said.

Savanna nodded. Personally, she thought her pony Coffee was the most beautiful, but this sure was one pretty pony!

"Oh, good. I was just about to come looking for you two," Miss Ellen said. "Sophia, meet your new pony, Piper."

Sophia gently reached out a hand. "Can I—"

But as she approached Piper, the pony pinned her ears back and snorted loudly.

Sophia dropped her hand. She knew that sound. It meant Piper wasn't happy.

"Maybe Piper just needs to get used to you!" Savanna said. "She's probably scared of new things."

Miss Ellen smiled a big smile. "Most of the other kids are too big to ride Piper, so she doesn't have a lot of riding experience. But don't worry. She'll warm up to you. You just need to go slow with her. Once you two get used to each other, I just know that you'll be a great rider for her, Sophia."

Sophia nodded. She really hoped Miss Ellen was right!

"Good," Miss Ellen said. "Now that's settled, can you take Piper to the barn?"

Sophia beamed. "Sure thing!" she said. "Come on, Piper. You'll see, I'm not so bad!"

All week, Sophia tried to make Piper see how kind she was. But despite her best efforts to be gentle, Piper still didn't trust her.

When she tried to pick Piper's hooves, the pony tried to kick her.

When she tried to put on Piper's bridle the pony raised her head high.

And when she tried to mount, Piper moved every time.

Sophia couldn't even get on her back to try riding her!

"You ready?" Savanna asked, poking her head into the barn Saturday morning. "Ms. Ellen is waiting for us."

Sophia looked up at Savanna . . . and burst into tears.

"What am I going to do?" Sophia cried. "She's just so…"

"Difficult?" Savanna finished the sentence.

"Yes!" She dropped her head down.

Savanna grinned and put a hand on her friend's shoulder. "Sounds like she's a little nervous. Kind of like someone else I know," she said and playfully nudged Sophia. "I'm sure you both just need time. It'll get better."

Sophia smiled softly and sighed. "I hope you're right. I'll never impress Miss Ellen if I can't even get on her." Wiping her tears, Sophia stood up. "We'd better get ready for the ring. Miss Ellen expects us to be on time."

As they neared the pasture, Savanna saw Coffee eagerly waiting for her.
"See you in the ring," she said, and turned toward her horse. Nodding, Sophia grabbed Piper's lead rope. But as she opened the gate to get Piper, the pony pinned her ears and took off running!

"Wait! Come back!" Sophia yelled, chasing after the pony. "Savanna! Help!"

The girls tripped and tumbled, slipped and stumbled, all around the pasture.

"She's . . . so . . . fast!" Sophia panted.

"Can't . . . keep . . . up!" Savanna wheezed.

Miss Ellen's dog Eli wriggled under the fence and chased after Piper, too.

In the other pasture, Coffee neighed as if to say, "Piper, stop running!"

"What's all the commotion?" Miss Ellen asked, entering the pasture. Then she saw the wild chase going on.

"ELI!" she yelled.

Eli immediately stopped and ducked under the fence into Coffee's pasture. Miss Ellen shook a pail of grain and Piper came trotting over.

"REALLY?!" Sophia put her hands on her hips but couldn't hold back the laughter.

Savanna and Miss Ellen couldn't either.

"Girls work smarter, not harder," Miss Ellen said. She stroked Piper on the neck and handed the lead rope to Sophia. "Ready to jump?"

Sophia gulped, a pit forming in her stomach. She and Piper hadn't been getting along. Could she really practice jumps on a pony who didn't trust her?

Savanna could tell that her friend was still nervous. As they walked, she put her arm around Sophia's and gave her a confident smile. "You've got this," she whispered.

Coffee neighed and Eli barked in agreement.

Sophia led Piper to the mounting block and tried to mount, but the pony kept moving just out of reach.

"Here, let me," Savanna said. She gently guided Piper closer to the mounting block and held her steady while Sophia tried again.

"Good girl," Sophia said, gently petting Piper's neck. "Good girl. Don't worry, you'll be great."
Piper seemed to relax at Sophia's gentle touch. She took a deep breath and then led Piper around the ring for a warmup.

The two cantered for a bit, getting used to each other. Then Miss Ellen called for them to jump.

Sophia closed her eyes. This was it. The moment of truth. What if Piper refused to jump?

But Piper knew what to do. The pony soared over the first jump and landed gracefully.

Sophia opened her eyes. "You did it, Piper! Good girl!" she said, giving the pony a quick pat. In the distance, she noticed Savanna cheering her on.

Pride filled up Sophia's chest at having finished the first jump. Suddenly, she wasn't worried. She wasn't scared. She was ready!

"Come on, Piper. We can do this," she said.

And, taking control of Piper's reins, the two navigated the course together.

"You both did great!" Savanna announced when they were done.

"You rode well, Sophia," Miss Ellen said with a smile. "Just imagine where you'll be with more practice!"

Sophia's heart raced with excitement. "I think you were right all along, Miss Ellen."

"Piper and I . . . we make a great team!"

# About the author

S. McMichael

Inspired by *McMichael's daughter, the Happenstance Farms* series highlights real-life lessons and relationships of a child equestrian. This is the second book of the series, Happenstance Farms: *Catch That Pony*, which is based on the true story of a youngster's adaption to a new pony.

# Others books in the series